The Bully

Story by
Kathryn Sutherland

Illustrations by
Claire Bridge

Jack and I were waiting in line at the playground to buy our lunch.

"I'm having a hamburger, Cal," said Jack. "What are you having?"

I didn't answer him because I'd just seen the big bully from our school walking toward us. "Look who's coming, Jack," I said. "Let's get out of here!"

"No way!" exclaimed Jack. "We've been standing in line for ages. We need to buy some lunch. I'm not going to let that bully make me go hungry."

"Well, it's not you he's staring at, is it?" I muttered.

"No," said Jack. "Maybe it's the kid behind you he wants." Jack was trying to be helpful, but he sounded worried.

"Hey you, kid!" The bully's voice was loud and mean, and his lip curled up as he spoke.

Everyone turned around. They knew that tone of voice and they knew what it meant. Who was going to be the bully's victim today?

SNACKS

The bully was heading straight toward me with big heavy steps. I swallowed and looked down, pretending not to notice him. Maybe if I ignored him he'd pick on somebody else. But he stopped right in front of me. I could see his big shoes in front of mine. My shoes looked very small.

"Give me your lunch money, kid," he snarled.

My heart was thumping as I looked up into his face, high above mine. He was standing very close—too close. He was leaning right over me. I wished he would go away.

What would the bully do to me if I didn't give him my lunch money?

I took a step backward.

Jack grabbed my sleeve. His eyes told me to stay right where I was. I looked up to face the bully, feeling glad that Jack was by my side.

Everyone was silent. They were all watching to see what would happen next. I could feel their eyes on me, but all I could see was the bully. His big, mean face was looking right down at me. I was terrified.

"Come on, hand it over!" he bellowed. The bully looked around. He knew everyone was watching.

I thought of all the times I had seen him pick on other kids. I'd watched and had wanted to help, but didn't dare. I knew now that everyone wanted to help me, but couldn't. The bully might pick on them next if they did. Every person there was as scared as I was.

Suddenly I felt angry. Why should one horrible person make everyone else feel so scared? What could I do to stop him?

The bully shouted in my face. "Did you hear what I said, kid? I told you to give me your lunch money!"

I took a breath and pulled my shoulders back. "No," I said.

I wondered if my voice had worked when I opened my mouth, but it had. Everybody gasped. I knew they were wondering what the bully would do to me now.

Then I saw some kids smiling at me, and I could feel their silent cheers.

"What did you say?" said the bully. He looked confused. Nobody had ever said *no* to him before.

"I said *no*. I won't give you my lunch money." It was easier to say this time.

Just then, someone in the line said, "You tell him, Cal!"

Someone else gave a quiet whistle.

The bully puffed out his chest and looked around. Then he put his face right down in front of mine again. He spoke very slowly and snarled, "Do you know who I am?"

I knew everyone was looking at me, and I knew they were on my side. I felt confident now. I stood up straight and said, "Yes, I've seen you around. I've seen you picking on kids and taking their money. We've all seen it, too many times." Then I said it again. "No! I'm not giving you my lunch money."

I heard a loud clap coming from the back of the line. Then it really started. A large crowd was gathering around us. They were calling out and clapping, too.

"Yeah, leave us alone!"

"Bring your own money."

"Stop being such a bully!"

"Good for you, Cal! You tell him!"

The bully didn't know what to say. He just stood still, open-mouthed.

Then Jack helped out. In a firm voice, he said to the bully, "Excuse me. The line is moving up. We need to buy our lunch."

The bully just stood there as though he couldn't believe what was happening. He looked at the crowd, and then he quickly walked away.

I was very relieved. I hadn't really expected
him to go.

Jack grinned and gave me a pat on the back. "You were great!" he said.

"Do you think so? I was really scared, but I feel good now," I smiled.

"Yes!" replied Jack. "You stood up to him and looked him right in the eye. That made him back down. Now, do you still want some lunch?"

"I'm really hungry," I said. "I think I'll have two hamburgers today!"